W9-CFV-508

Komodo Dragons

Other titles in the Nature's Predators series include:

Komodo Dragons

Marcia S. Gresko

**KIDHAVEN
PRESS**™

THOMSON

™

GALE

San Diego • Detroit • New York • San Francisco • Cleveland
New Haven, Conn. • Waterville, Maine • London • Munich

© 2004 by KidHaven Press. KidHaven Press is an imprint of The Gale Group, Inc.,
a division of Thomson Learning, Inc.

KidHaven™ and Thomson Learning™ are trademarks used herein under license.

For more information, contact
KidHaven Press
27500 Drake Rd.
Farmington Hills, MI 48331-3535
Or you can visit our Internet site at http://www.gale.com

ALL RIGHTS RESERVED.
No part of this work covered by the copyright hereon may be reproduced or used in any form
or by any means—graphic, electronic, or mechanical, including photocopying, recording, taping,
Web distribution or information storage retrieval systems—without the written permission of
the publisher.

LIBRARY OF CONGRESS CATALOGING-IN-PUBLICATION DATA

Gresko, Marcia S.
  Komodo Dragons / by Marcia S. Gresko.
    p. cm. — (Nature's predators)
Summary: Discusses Komodo dragons including habitat, anatomy, hunting practices
and diet, conservation efforts, and captive-breeding programs.
Includes bibliographical references and index.
  ISBN 0-7377-1764-5 (hardback)
  1. Komodo dragon—Juvenile literature. [1. Komodo dragon. 2.
Lizards.] I. Title. II. Series.
  QL666.L29G74 2004
  597.95'968—dc21

2003003554

Printed in the United States of America

CONTENTS

CHAPTER ONE

Island King

Snug in a huge mound of twigs and dirt—the stolen nest of an island bird—lie twenty large, leathery eggs. The lizards inside the eggs have been growing for about eight months. Now they are ready to hatch.

Using a special "egg tooth" on the end of their snout, the **hatchlings** slash their way free from their shells. They emerge from the broken, three-inch shells and rest from their task. Curled among the bits of shell, the brightly colored four-ounce lizards are nearly eighteen inches long.

Startled by a crashing in a nearby thicket, the little lizards scurry up the nearest tree to safety—just in time. A Komodo dragon, the island's fierce ruler, springs from the brush. The giant lizard is looking for a meal, and baby lizards—even though they are his own kind—make a tasty snack.

But the tiny dragons are too quick, and the island king continues its hunt.

Predator on the Prowl

The Komodo dragon rules a small kingdom of several islands in Indonesia. Located in Southeast Asia
between the Pacific Ocean and the Indian Ocean, Indonesia is a group of more than seventeen thousand
islands. The Komodo dragon regularly roams just a
handful of these islands: Flores, Rinca, Gili Motang,
and Komodo, after which it is named. But the dragons are strong swimmers, and they sometimes visit
other islands to hunt.

Komodo dragons are predators, animals that kill
and eat other animals. All Komodo dragons are **carnivores**. But their meal choice depends on the
dragon's age and the kinds of prey that are available.

Hatchlings live in trees, sleeping in holes or
under loose bark, for the first few years of their lives.
Their leafy nurseries are well stocked with food.

Young Komodo dragons live in trees. Once they grow to three or four feet long, they live on the ground.

Snapping up insects of all kinds, the young dragons grow quickly, doubling their weight in a year. Soon they are ready for larger meals, including eggs, baby birds, and tree-dwelling lizards called geckos.

Once **juveniles** grow about three to four feet long, they are too big and heavy for their treetop homes. They must leave them to live and stalk their prey on the ground. Birds and rodents, such as rats and mice, are on the menu.

Adult Komodo dragons eat any animal they can find and kill. Deer and wild boar are their favorite prey. Adult dragons also regularly attack animals as big as or much bigger than themselves, such as wild horses and water buffalo. But they feed on smaller animals as well, such as birds, wild dogs, monkeys, and snakes, including poisonous ones. On a visit to the beach, adult dragons dig up and devour sea turtle and saltwater crocodile eggs. They catch turtle and crocodile hatchlings, adult turtles, fish, and crabs.

Adult Komodo dragons are also **cannibals**. Almost 10 percent of an adult dragon's diet is made up of other dragons. Adult dragons feed mainly on live young dragons or on the **carcasses** of old dragons.

Humans are sometimes attacked and even killed and eaten by Komodo dragons. But despite the terrifying tales, dragons have killed fewer than twenty people in the last one hundred years. Even though hungry adult dragons often raid local villages, dragging off goats and gobbling up chickens and pet animals, villagers report that they are easily driven off with a large stick.

Scary Scavengers

In addition to eating fresh meat, both juvenile and adult dragons are greedy **scavengers**. Komodo dragons are not picky eaters. Attracted by the foul odor of a rotting carcass, the determined dragons move directly toward dinner. When they find their smelly meal, they feast on the spoiling meat squirming with worms and maggots.

Finding **carrion**, or dead animal flesh, takes less energy than hunting prey, and dragons feed eagerly

Komodo dragons are not picky eaters. They will head straight for a rotting carcass for a meal.

Komodo dragons are the world's largest lizards. Males can reach up to ten feet long and weigh over three hundred pounds.

---

on most dead animals they find. The giant lizards have even been known to visit cemeteries to dig up human **corpses** to satisfy their hunger. The dragon's huge appetite matches its enormous body.

A Real-Life Legend

The Komodo dragon is the world's largest lizard. Males average seven to eight feet long. Females are usually smaller, growing five to seven feet long. The largest Komodo dragon on record was a male slightly over ten feet long from snout to tail, about the length of a small car. Female dragons weigh about one hundred and fifty pounds. Large males may weigh nearly three hundred pounds—on an empty stomach.

An adult Komodo dragon can eat up to 80 percent of its own body weight in a single meal. A three-hundred-pound male may weigh more than five hundred pounds after gorging on a banquet-sized buffalo. After such a bonanza, the bloated dragon may not eat again for weeks, although it may snack on smaller prey such as birds, dogs, and even porcupine.

Feast-or-Fast Lifestyle

Adult dragons eat only about twelve mammoth meals a year. Dragons can thrive on this feast-or-fast lifestyle because they are cold-blooded. Warm-blooded carnivores, such as wolves and lions, heat their bodies with the energy from food. Dragons, however, keep warm by **basking** in the hot sun. They cool down by finding a shady spot. This energy-efficient way of controlling their body temperature means that dragons require much less food than their fellow predators. In fact, an adult dragon may be able to live on only 10 percent of the amount a same-sized predator needs. Even a large Komodo dragon can survive on an average of just a pound of food per day.

Dragons rarely have leftovers. Lions may leave 25 to 30 percent of their kill uneaten. Dragons devour about 90 percent of their prey, from horns to hooves. Trampled, bloodstained grass, a few wisps of hair, and the contents of its victim's stomach are usually the only signs that a dragon has eaten dinner.

Smart Senses

Before a dragon can dine, it must first find its meal. A dragon's primary food-finding tool is its vomeronasal sense. This sense is a combination of smell and taste.

Swinging its huge head from side to side, a dragon flicks its long, forked yellow tongue through a notch at the front of its lower jaw. The darting tongue picks up scent particles from the air. As the dragon's tongue retreats into its mouth, it places these particles on a small organ on the roof of the mouth. This organ, called the Jacobson's organ, "smells" the dragon's dinner by recognizing the scent particles. If the wind is right, Komodo dragons can smell a stinky carrion dinner up to 6.75 miles away.

A dragon's sense of sight also helps it hunt. Dragons can see objects nearly a thousand feet away. Their large brown eyes are quick to pick up any slight movement on the horizon or in the thickets in which they prowl for prey.

Terrible Teeth and Deadly Drool

A dragon's teeth are its deadliest weapons for catching and killing its next meal. Dragons have sixty teeth, nearly twice as many as humans do. Sharp and curved, dragons' teeth resemble those of a shark or dinosaur.

Notched like a saw on the back edge, the teeth are arranged in a gradual curve. This shape, similar to a surgeon's scalpel, makes the dragon's teeth powerful meat carvers. The teeth break off easily and are replaced often. A dragon may grow more than two hundred new teeth a year.

Rotting bits of meat from the dragon's last meal cling to its jagged teeth. **Bacteria** live in these leftovers. A dragon's saliva contains more than fifty dif-

Komodo dragons have sixty razor-sharp teeth that they use to catch and kill prey.

ferent types of bacteria. At least four of the types can cause blood poisoning. Thus, even if an injured animal escapes a dragon's terrible teeth, its wounds usually become **lethal**. Just a nip from a dragon can cause infection. The injured animal usually dies within a few days, becoming food for its attacker or for other scavenging dragons.

Smart Lizards

Catching and killing **fleet-footed** prey is hard work for slow-moving dragons. Dragons have to be smart to survive. The Komodo dragon is one of the smarter members of the lizard family. Dragons regularly bask high on hills where they can smell and track the rotting carcasses of escaped meals. Dragons also remember where they have caught food before and regularly check those spots for second helpings. They keep track of pregnant goats and horses, too. Being nearby when the animals give birth often means an easy two-course meal of a helpless mother and newborn.

Komodo dragons are powerful and smart. They have keen senses, knifelike teeth, and lethal saliva. This combination makes the Komodo dragon the island king.

CHAPTER TWO

The Hunt

Located close to the equator, the Komodo dragon's kingdom is warm all year. From December through March, monsoon winds bring heavy rains. From April to November, it is hot and dry. The islands' landscape varies from rugged peaks to grasslands and forests. It is a harsh, dangerous place.

Deadly snakes slither through the tall grass. Poisonous spiders dart among the rocks. In the surrounding waters, currents swiftly change, whirlpools, spin, and hungry sharks lurk. Towering tidal waves batter the shores. Active volcanoes on neighboring islands explode, blanketing the dragon's domain with choking dust and ash.

Hunting Grounds

Komodo dragons know their hazardous home well. Each dragon has a home range that is made up of

Komodo dragons live on several islands in Indonesia including Komodo Island (pictured).

three types of activity areas. The largest of these areas is the scavenging area. In this area the dragon locates carrion meals. In the smaller foraging area, the dragon hunts for food. The dragon spends most of its time in the core area, the smallest zone. The core area contains burrows and other sleeping places, basking spots, and sites the dragon uses to **ambush** its prey.

The size of a Komodo dragon's home range depends on the size of the dragon. The bigger the dragon, the bigger the home range it prowls. Male dragons have a larger home range than female dragons. Because its home range may be vast, a dragon does not defend its territory the way some predators, such as wolves, do. In fact, a dragon's scavenging and foraging areas often overlap with those of a neighbor. However, dragons do mark their ambushing stations, sleeping and basking sites, and hunting trails with **dung**. These smelly signs warn other dragons to avoid these areas.

Some adult dragons may occupy their home range for twenty-five to forty years. They discover every watering hole, nesting area, resting place, and game trail. This enables the dragons to learn the best places to hunt.

Hunting Made Easy

Komodo dragons want the hunt to be as easy as possible. Large adult dragons regularly kill animals twice their own weight. They are capable of killing animals ten to fifteen times their size. But they prefer easier game, animals that are young, old, or sick. A helpless fawn or boar piglet, a water buffalo slowed by age, or a lame deer make perfect targets.

What seems bloodthirsty is actually useful. When dragons kill weak animals, the rest of the population

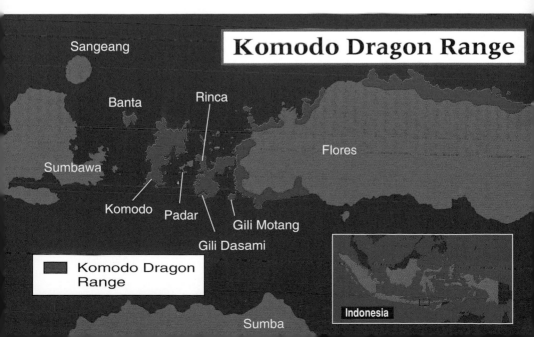

becomes stronger. Controlling a species' population also means that its members are less likely to starve or destroy their habitat. In addition, killing sick animals helps prevent other animals from getting ill. Dragons—and their big appetites—are one way nature keeps the islands' ecosystem in balance.

Hunting Strategies

How dragons hunt depends on the type of prey. Hunting for insects, young dragons move quickly

---

Large Komodo dragons can kill prey twice their own weight and many times their own size.

through the grass. When the bugs land on nearby grass blades, the dragons snap them up. Dragons in search of a lizard lunch scour the trees. They flick their tongues under slabs of loose bark and poke their heads in every crack and hole they find. Rodents, such as rats, are often dug out of their burrows under logs and trash. Birds of all kinds are also frequently on the menu. Dragons know where many bird species nest, and they visit these places regularly for easy egg meals. Dragons usually devour the adult birds while the birds feed on the ground.

Bigger, faster meals require a different hunting strategy. Dragons can run at speeds of about ten miles an hour. But fleet-footed deer dash off at fifty miles an hour, and wild horses gallop away at forty miles per hour. Therefore, hungry dragons do not chase these large, speedy prey. Instead, they mainly use two other hunting methods: **stealth** and ambush. Using stealth, a dragon carefully sneaks up on unsuspecting prey, such as sleeping deer or nesting birds. Using ambush, a hidden dragon waits for its prey to come to it.

Big Game Hide-and-Seek

A dragon's hunting day begins early. Waking at dawn, the dragon moves directly to a sunny spot to bask. After warming up, it tests the air with its long, yellow tongue. If it catches the scent of carrion, it sets out for an easy, ready-to-eat meal. If not, it is ready to hunt. Morning is prime time for hunting one of the dragon's favorite meals, deer.

Following a familiar game trail, the dragon selects an ambush site. The best place for an ambush is along a trail that deer often use. To increase its chance of success, the dragon chooses a spot where several trails merge. Next the dragon clears a space for itself about the size of its body. It tramples down the tall grass and pushes away the loose sticks and stones. Then the dragon lies flat on the ground, its head low and stretched forward. Motionless, except for the flicking of its long yellow tongue, the dragon waits. Its clay-colored skin helps it blend in with its surroundings.

Several hours may pass, but the dragon is patient. It knows its prey's schedule. Deer are mostly **nocturnal**. They graze in the grasslands at night when the dragon is asleep. At dawn, they move to nearby hilltops to rest and digest their food. When the hot island sun sears the hilltops, the deer move down the trails to the cool, shady forests to sleep.

If the dragon's carefully planned ambush fails, it has another chance later in the day. Afternoon is the perfect time to switch to stealth tactics. The dragon knows the bushes and thickets where the deer usually sleep, and it will drag the slumbering creatures to their death from these hiding places.

If the dragon gets lucky, though, a few hot, tired deer make their way down the trail. The dragon continues to crouch calmly. It waits quietly for the deer to get within striking range. When its intended victim is just a few feet away, the dragon charges.

A Komodo dragon waits patiently to ambush its next meal. Dragons are slow and must ambush fast-moving prey.

Attacking the animal's feet first, the dragon knocks the deer to the ground. Struggling wildly, the terrified deer staggers upright. Before it can bound away, the dragon lunges again. It clasps the deer by the throat with its serrated teeth. Clamping its strong jaws around the deer's throat, it begins to shake its prey violently from side to side. This time the deer goes down for good. Badly injured and in shock, the deer lies still. Then the dragon launches the final attack—slashing open the deer's belly. The animal quickly bleeds to death, and the dragon begins to feed.

CHAPTER THREE

Mealtime

D ragon dining is bloody business. A dragon usually begins to eat by ripping open its victim's belly to get at the soft internal organs, or viscera, inside. First it pulls out the deer's stomach and intestines. Slinging them from side to side, the dragon empties their contents—its prey's undigested food—before devouring the stomach and intestines. Next the deer's **diaphragm** is pulled out and eaten. Then, thrusting its head deep into the deer's body, the dragon yanks out the lungs, heart, and other organs. Snapping its jaws noisily, the dragon bolts down these fatty, nutrition-packed portions. But these tasty treats are just the first course.

The Main Course

The dragon then turns its attention to the rest of its meal. Sinking its sharp teeth into the carcass, the dragon plants its muscular legs far apart. Then it rocks back and forth, throwing its weight into each backward movement. Using this sawing motion, the dragon slices off huge hunks of the deer's flesh. A Komodo dragon's teeth are made for tearing, not chewing, so it gulps these meaty chunks down whole. Dragons have been reported to swallow the entire hindquarter of a full-grown goat or a whole month-old fawn in a single mouthful.

Komodo dragons use their teeth for ripping and tearing, and they swallow large parts of their prey whole.

Komodo dragons have movable joints in their jaws that allow them to open their mouths wide and swallow large pieces of meat.

To allow these mammoth mouthfuls to go down, a dragon's skull has a special design. Movable joints enable the dragon to stretch its jaws unusually wide. The lower jaw can also be shifted backward and forward, which helps the dragon pull large pieces of meat into its mouth.

Thick gobs of saliva also allow the dragon's food to slide down its throat more easily. As the dragon feeds, its saliva turns almost red from its *own* blood.

About two-thirds of a Komodo dragon's razor-sharp teeth are buried in its spongy gums. When the dragon bites into its prey's flesh, the gums are pushed back, baring these clever carving utensils. Sometimes the dragon's soft gums are cut against the jagged edges of its teeth as the dragon bites and tears at its meal.

The dragon eats quickly. One researcher saw a ninety-pound dragon eat a sixty-eight-pound boar in just seventeen minutes. A large dragon can gobble down as much as five and a half pounds of meat per minute. This is faster than any other predator, except some large snakes. Speed eating is an important survival strategy. The faster the dragon eats, the more food it will keep for itself. Other dragons are quick to catch the scent of a fresh kill. When they do, they immediately invite themselves for dinner.

Dinner Guests

Within several hours of a kill, a dinner party of three to four dragons is common. Because Komodo dragons live and hunt alone, this gathering is tense. Large dragons hiss at each other, inflating the pouches in their throats, mouths gaping wide. Their bodies held high, their necks arched, and their tails lashing from side to side, each dragon is ready to strike. If the face-off continues, one of the opponents may lunge and bite the other or inflict a blow with its tail. Fighting dragons may get up on their hind legs and grasp one another with their arms. Locked in combat, the weaker dragon tries to break free and run. The win-

Dragons often feed together on one kill. The dominant dragon usually eats most of the meat.

ner may give chase, forcing the loser to the ground, and paw it with its sharp claws.

However, the biggest dragon's threatening manner is usually enough to show others who is in charge of the feast. Wise dragons just move out of this **dominant** dragon's way. The large dragon takes the choice morsels, the best position at the carcass, and the most food.

Smaller dragons also try to make themselves welcome at the feast. Walking with a slow, stiff-legged gait, a young dragon circles the group. It keeps its mouth shut and its head down. This meek manner shows the larger dragons that the small one knows its place and will only take a turn at the leftovers. Sometimes young dragons roll in the intestinal contents of the dead animal. Because dragons do not eat their victim's intestinal contents, some scientists think this protects the smaller dragons from being the next item on the menu.

As the cluster of dragons feeds, individual dragons move about. Some rest in the shade between snack breaks. Others use the gathering as an opportunity to look for possible mates.

Depending on the dinner's size, the meal may be over in just a few hours. Four big dragons were reported to devour a large deer in less than four hours. Studies have shown that several adult dragons can eat a twenty-six-hundred-pound water buffalo in three to five days. And nearly the entire carcass is consumed—head, hide, hooves, and bones.

The Leftovers

After gorging on so much food, a dragon's belly often drags on the ground. Slowly, it moves off to find a watering hole. The dragon plunges its head into the water, up to its eyes, and drinks deeply. Then it drags itself to a sunny spot to bask and digest its huge dinner. It may take a dragon anywhere from four days to several weeks to digest a meal. Warmed by the sun, the dragon's digestive system works more efficiently, helping the dragon to digest its meal more quickly. This prevents the food from rotting in the dragon's bloated belly and poisoning it.

Strong acids in the dragon's stomach break down food to be used by its body. But the Komodo dragon cannot digest every part of the animals it eats. Although a dragon consumes its entire prey, it does not digest bones, teeth, hooves, claws, hair, or feathers. The skin of reptiles, the skin and legs of birds, and bird and reptile eggshells are also rarely digested.

Komodo dragons nap after a big meal. The dragon's digestive system works best when the animal is warmed by the sun.

Instead, the dragon coughs up these leftovers in a mass called a gastric pellet. Made up of mostly matted hair glued together with vile-smelling mucus, pellets may contain items as big as the jaw and skull of a wild boar. One large pellet contained the remains of at least two meals: the hair of a goat and the hooves, neck bones, and tusks of a boar. The pellet measured nearly eighteen inches long and four inches in diameter.

To vomit up one of these pellets, a dragon stands high on all four legs. With body and neck arched up off the ground, it extends its neck and opens its mouth wide. Then it pulls its stomach in and throws its head from side to side. If the pellet is small, the slimy "hair ball" may be thrown a great distance. If the pellet is large, the dragon backs up and away from the messy mass as it slides from its mouth. Then it rubs its face in the dirt or brush and cleans its lips with its tongue. Most gastric pellets are thrown up in the early morning. Then the giant lizard prepares to hunt again.

CHAPTER FOUR

Dragons in Danger

Even an island king faces dangers. Fierce wild boar and angry twelve-hundred-pound water buffalo are perilous prey. Dragons often bear scars from the slashing tusks and strong hooves of these victims.

Dragons also face starvation because they compete with other animals for food. Birds, dogs, and civet cats share about half their menu choices with dragons. Some dragons starve, especially in the long dry season when prey is scarce.

Dying Young

Young dragons lead especially risky lives. Adult Komodo dragons are at the top of the islands' food chain. This means they kill and eat many other animals but no other animals prey on them.

Young dragons, however, have yet to become these awesome killers. Dogs, civet cats, snakes, flesh-eating birds, and wild boar regularly eat young dragons. Boar also destroy many dragon nests. But the greatest danger to young dragons does not come from other predators; it comes from fellow dragons. The danger begins even before the baby dragons are born.

About a month after a male and female dragon mate, the female lays her eggs. She may remain near the nest for as long as two months. Then she wanders off. Her duties as a parent are over, and her **offspring** must fend for themselves for the rest of their lives.

Until the eggs hatch about six months later, the tiny dragons growing inside have no protection. Both male and female dragons dig up and eat the eggs of their own kind. Hungry parents may even kill their own offspring.

A female dragon emerges from her burrow after laying eggs. She will leave the nest for good before the eggs hatch.

To prevent becoming an adult dragon's dinner, newly hatched dragons scramble up nearby trees. The young dragons keep to their tree house shelters for a year or more. Once they have grown between three and four feet long, the dragons descend to the ground. This is a dangerous time. The juvenile is too bulky for treetop life but not big and fast enough to escape a determined adult. Cannibalism is a constant threat for juvenile dragons.

Homegrown Dangers

Even the strongest adult dragon is no match for the violent natural disasters that rock its island home. The Komodo dragon's habitat is located inside what scientists call the Ring of Fire, an area famous for shattering earthquakes and fiery volcanoes.

In many parts of Indonesia, the earth trembles every few weeks. The country also has about 220 active volcanoes. More than a dozen of them tower over Flores Island, where many dragons live. When a volcano erupts, explosions, wildfires, and tidal waves may threaten everything on the island.

Natural disasters in their habitat endanger the Komodo dragon's survival. There are only three thousand to five thousand Komodo dragons left in the wild. All of them live in an area of less than five hundred square miles. This is the smallest range of any large carnivore. When all the members of a species live close together like dragons do, the entire species is at risk. A natural disaster could wipe out all of an island's dragons.

A volcano towers over a village on Indonesia's Flores Island. Active volcanoes are a danger to Komodo dragons.

The Human Threat

Dragons have to share their small home with people, too. Indonesia is a country with a very large and growing population. This population growth is a serious threat to dragon survival. More people mean less room for the giant lizards. In once-empty wilderness areas, people have built villages and settled farms. As forests are cleared and grasslands planted with crops, the dragons' already tiny territory shrinks even more.

People also kill the food that dragons rely on, especially deer and wild boar. To flush deer and other animals from the thick brush, **poachers** often set fires. Some scientists believe that fires and the uncontrolled hunting of deer helped lead to the extinction of dragons on another Indonesian island, Padar Island.

When their hunting grounds disappear and their natural prey are killed by human hunters, hungry dragons kill what is available: livestock and other farm animals. In response, villagers sometimes hunt the dragons. They may also poison carrion that dragons feed on.

Conservation Efforts

Aware that the magnificent dragons are in danger, the Indonesian government has taken steps to protect them. In 1980, the government made Komodo and several nearby islands a national park. Many animals are protected in the park, including Komodo dragons and their prey species—deer, wild buffalo, and boar.

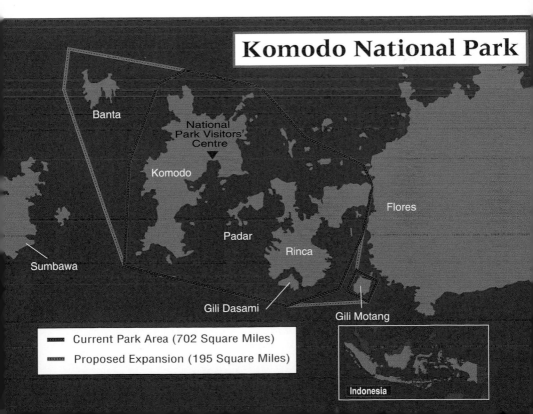

Komodo National Park

Banta

National Park Visitors' Centre

Komodo

Flores

Padar

Rinca

Sumbawa

Gili Dasami

Gili Motang

▬▬▬ Current Park Area (702 Square Miles)
▬▬▬ Proposed Expansion (195 Square Miles)

Indonesia

But not all dragons live in Komodo National Park. Though it is illegal to hunt or kill the dragons anywhere, those outside the park's guarded boundaries are still in grave danger from humans. The dragons on unprotected Flores Island continue to face trouble. Settlers slash and burn the dragon's forest habitat and compete with the dragons for food.

Researchers and conservationists have stepped in to help the government's efforts to save the dragons. Convincing settlers to view the Komodo dragon as a precious resource rather than a hungry pest is an important first step. The dragons already draw thousands of visitors to the islands each year. Enabling settlers to share the dollars that visitors spend may persuade them to live alongside their dragon neighbors in peace.

Another way to encourage islanders to safeguard the dragons is to involve them in the conservation effort. Scientists have set up programs for local students to participate in dragon research studies. Working in these programs helps students understand the lizards better. Students also learn skills that they can use to get good jobs in wildlife conservation. These homegrown experts will be responsible for protecting the dragons and their habitat in the future.

Finally, scientists suggest ways people can live without destroying the dragons' habitat. For example, settlers can grow bamboo or make bricks for use in building. This will save forests from being cleared for lumber.

Approximately three hundred Komodo dragons live in zoos around the world, and captive-breeding programs ensure their survival.

Captive-Breeding Programs

Zoos around the world also help keep Komodo dragons safe. Approximately three hundred captive dragons live in zoos in Indonesia, North America, Europe, Asia, and Australia. Breeding programs at these zoos ensure that the Komodo dragon will never become extinct, even if the natural population is wiped out.

Captive dragons also provide an educational opportunity for zoo visitors who would never have the chance to see dragons in the wild. Zoo exhibits and programs can increase public understanding of the dragons and support for saving them.

Captive dragons may be returned to the wild one day. Dragons have been extinct on Padar Island for more than two decades. Dragons are disappearing in areas of Flores Island, as well. Captive dragons might someday be released to live in such places again.

In Human Hands

The future of the Komodo dragon in the wild is uncertain. But research scientists work hard to keep it bright. They spend long, hot, sometimes dangerous hours in the field studying the dragons. Sometimes they trap the creatures and fit them with radio harnesses. This special equipment sends out a signal that tells the scientists where the dragons are at all times. By tracking dragons, researchers discover new facts about them. What they learn will hopefully help the dragons not only survive but thrive.

GLOSSARY

ambush: To hide and then attack.

bacteria: Germs.

bask: To lie in the sun.

cannibal: An animal that eats its own kind.

carcass: The body of a dead animal.

carnivore: An animal that eats mainly meat.

carrion: Dead animal flesh.

corpse: The body of a dead human.

diaphragm: A muscle that helps the lungs expand and contract.

dominant: To be in charge; the dominant dragon is usually the largest dragon.

dung: Animal waste product or feces.

fleet-footed: Able to run fast.

hatchling: A baby.

juvenile: An animal that has not yet become sexually mature.

lethal: Deadly.

nocturnal: Active at night.

offspring: An animal's young.

poacher: Someone who hunts illegally.

scavenger: An animal that feeds on dead animals.

stealth: A hunting technique in which the dragon sneaks up on its prey.

Books

Kathy Darling, *Komodo Dragon: On Location*. New York: Lothrop, Lee & Shepard Books, 1997. This book describes the physical characteristics, behavior, and habitat of the Komodo dragon, as well as the dangers facing it.

James Martin, *Komodo Dragons: Giant Lizards of Indonesia*. Mankato, MN: Capstone Press, 1995. Part of the publisher's Animals and the Environment series, this book explains the Komodo dragon's status as an endangered animal and efforts to protect it.

Anne Welsbacher, *Komodo Dragons*. Mankato, MN: Capstone Press, 2002. This book provides information about the physical characteristics, habitat, and hunting habits of the Komodo dragon and includes a "fast facts" section.

Periodical

Fiona Sunquist, "The Lizard Kings," *National Geographic World*, November 1995. Describes the characteristics of the Komodo dragon, including a section of "strange but true facts."

Websites

Honolulu Zoo (www.honoluluzoo.org). This site includes a video of baby Komodo dragons and basic information on dragon characteristics and behavior.

Komodo National Park (www.komodonational park.org). This is the official site of Indonesia's national Komodo dragon preserve. There is a fact sheet, photo gallery, answers to frequently asked questions, and links to additional information.

Los Angeles Zoo "Dragons of Komodo" (www.lazoo. org). A fact sheet and photo gallery of pictures taken at the zoo's Dragons of Komodo exhibit.

Woodland Park Zoo (www.zoo.org). This site has answers to frequently asked questions about Komodo dragons and an excellent fact sheet that includes information on their habitat, physical characteristics, life cycle, and conservation.

INDEX

PICTURE CREDITS

Cover Image: © The Image Bank
Jose Azel/Aurora, 15
Sara-Jane Cleland/Lonely Planet Images, 18
© Corel, 20
© Tui De Roy/Minden Pictures, 6, 27, 31, 34
© Gavriel Jecan/CORBIS, 23
© Mark Jones/Minden Pictures, 12
Chris Jouan, 8, 19, 37
© Wolfgang Kaehler/CORBIS, 29, 36, 39
© 2002 Jim Kern Expeditions, 9
© Charles & Josette Lenars/CORBIS, 11, 26

ABOUT THE AUTHOR

Marcia S. Gresko has written more than twenty non-fiction books for young readers, including *Tide Pools, Wolves,* and *The Medieval Castle* for KidHaven Press. A former teacher for fifteen years, she holds a B.A. in English from the State University of New York at Buffalo and an M.A. in education from the University of Rochester. Gresko lives with her husband and daughter in Southern California.